Awful, Disgusting Parasites

I0884208

TICKS

MARGARET MINCKS

BLACK RABBIT BOOKS

Bolt is published by Black Rabbit Books
P.O. Box 3263, Mankato, Minnesota, 56002.
www.blackrabbitbooks.com
Copyright © 2017 Black Rabbit Books

Design and Production by Michael Sellner
Photo Research by Rhonda Milbrett

All rights reserved. No part of this book may be reproduced in any form without written permission from the publisher.

Library of Congress Control Number: 2015954683

HC ISBN: 978-1-68072-011-2 PB ISBN: 978-1-68072-275-8

Printed in the United States at CG Book Printers, North Mankato, Minnesota, 56003. PO #1792 4/16

Web addresses included in this book were working and appropriate at the time of publication. The publisher is not responsible for broken or changed links.

Image Credits

Corbis: David Scharf, Cover; Dreamstime: Jenheltonphoto, 25 (left); istock: Astrid Gast, 14 (top), 31; Henrik_L, 6–7; olikim, 16, 22; RolfAasa, 11; Masato Hattori, 28–29; Science Source: 12 (bottom), 21, 25 (right); Eye of Science, 8 (left), 26; Shutterstock: 3drenderings, 24; Cosmin Manci, 8 (right); Designua, 18; evgdemidova, 27; Henrik Larsson, 10, 12 (top), 15 (both); irin-k, 9; Risto0, Back Cover, 1, 4–5, 14–15 (background); Sarah2, 14 (bottom), 20–21; Smileus, 3, 23; Vitalii Hulai, 32; yingphoto, 17
Every effort has been made to contact copyright holders for material reproduced in this book. Any omissions will be rectified in subsequent printings if notice is given to the publisher.

Contents

CHAPTER 1

Tricky Ticks

Hiding in tall grass, a tick waits. Soon, a hiker comes by. The tiny, sneaky critter climbs up the hiker's sock. It's thirsty for blood.

Ticks are **parasites**. Parasites live in or on plants or other animals. Ticks drink blood from any animal. Their small, flat bodies make them hard to find.

TICK BODY PARTS

HEAD
FEEDING TUBE
MOUTH

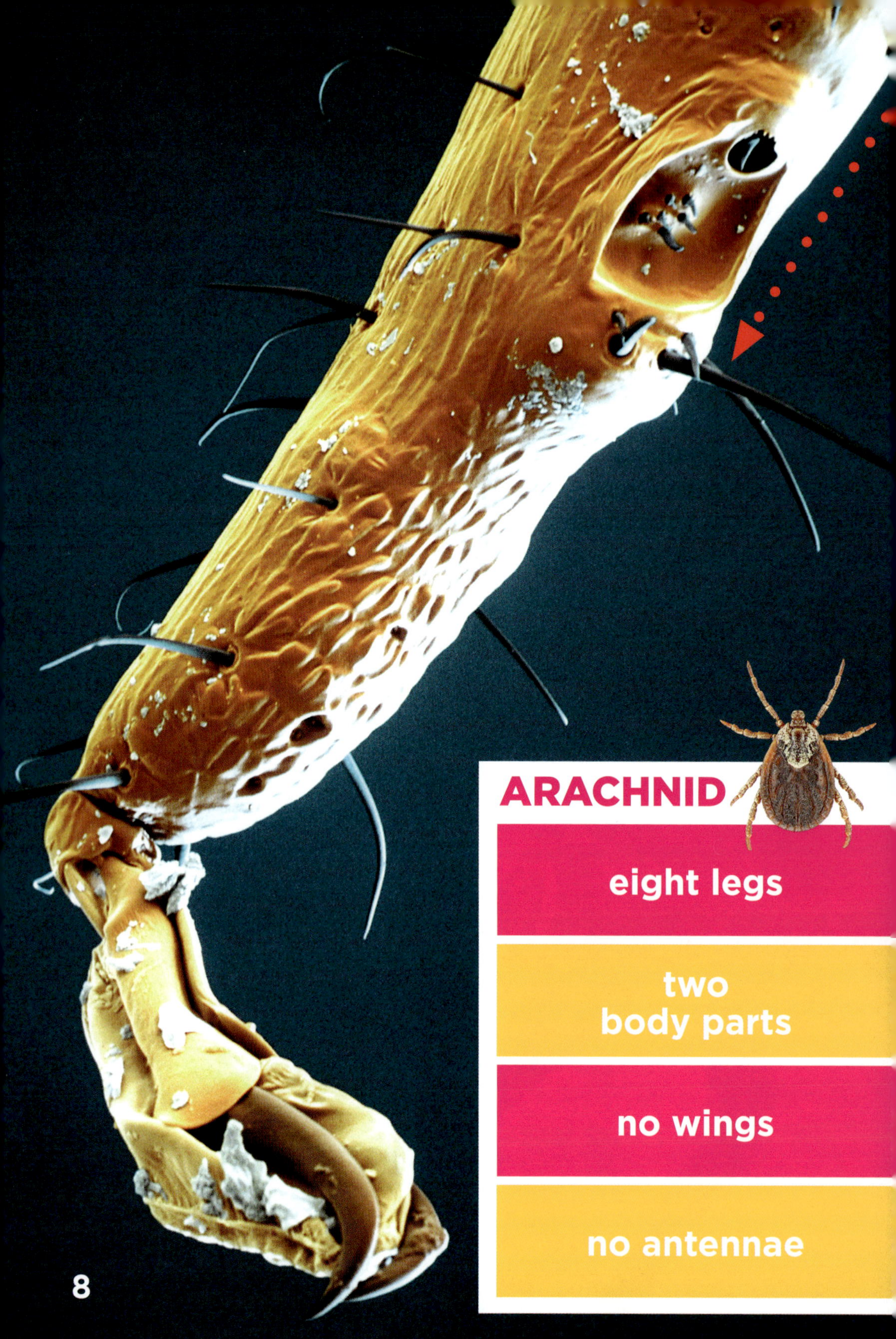

ARACHNID

eight legs
two body parts
no wings
no antennae

Not an Insect!

Even though ticks bug us, they're not insects. They're actually related to spiders. Ticks' legs have short **spines** and tiny claws. These claws help ticks grab their meals. Once they grab on, ticks use feeding tubes to drink blood.

INSECT

- six legs
- three body parts
- wings (most of the time)
- antennae

ARACHNID OR INSECT?

CHAPTER 2

A Tick's Life

More than 800 kinds of ticks roam the world. Ticks live up to three years. They start their lives as eggs. After eating, female ticks lay eggs. The eggs hatch in about a month or two. After hatching, ticks become **larvae**.

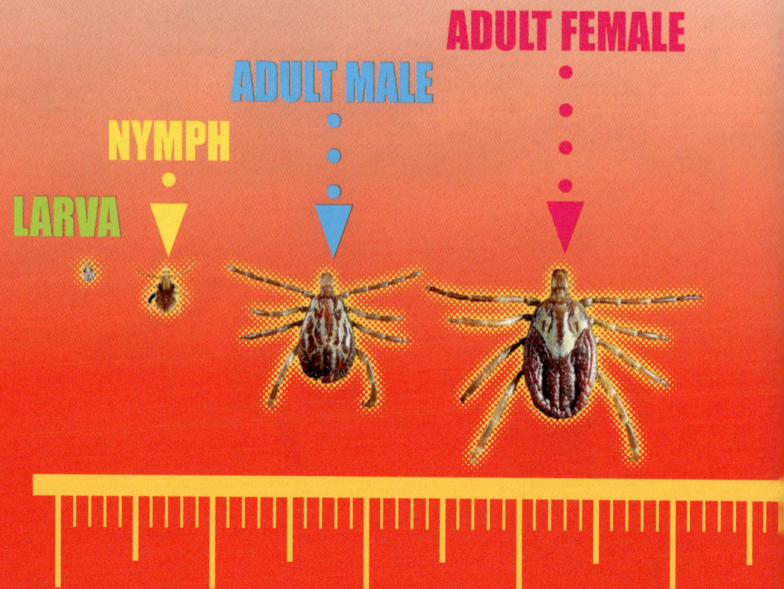
ADULT FEMALE
ADULT MALE
NYMPH
LARVA

From Larvae to Adults

Larvae have only six legs. These young ticks spend their time on the forest floor. They feed on small animals. Larvae grow and shed their **exoskeletons**.

After shedding, larvae become nymphs. Nymphs look like small adult ticks. They have eight legs. Nymphs feed on humans or small animals as they grow into adults.

A TICK'S SMALL WORLD

FEMALE TICK
LAYS EGGS

ADULT TICK

SIX-LEGGED LARVA
EIGHT-LEGGED NYMPH

CHAPTER 3

Carrying Diseases

Ticks spread more diseases than any other bloodsucking creatures. Ticks feed on animals. Sometimes those animals carry diseases. Ticks pick up illnesses when drinking sick animals' blood. Then, when they bite other animals, they pass the diseases on.

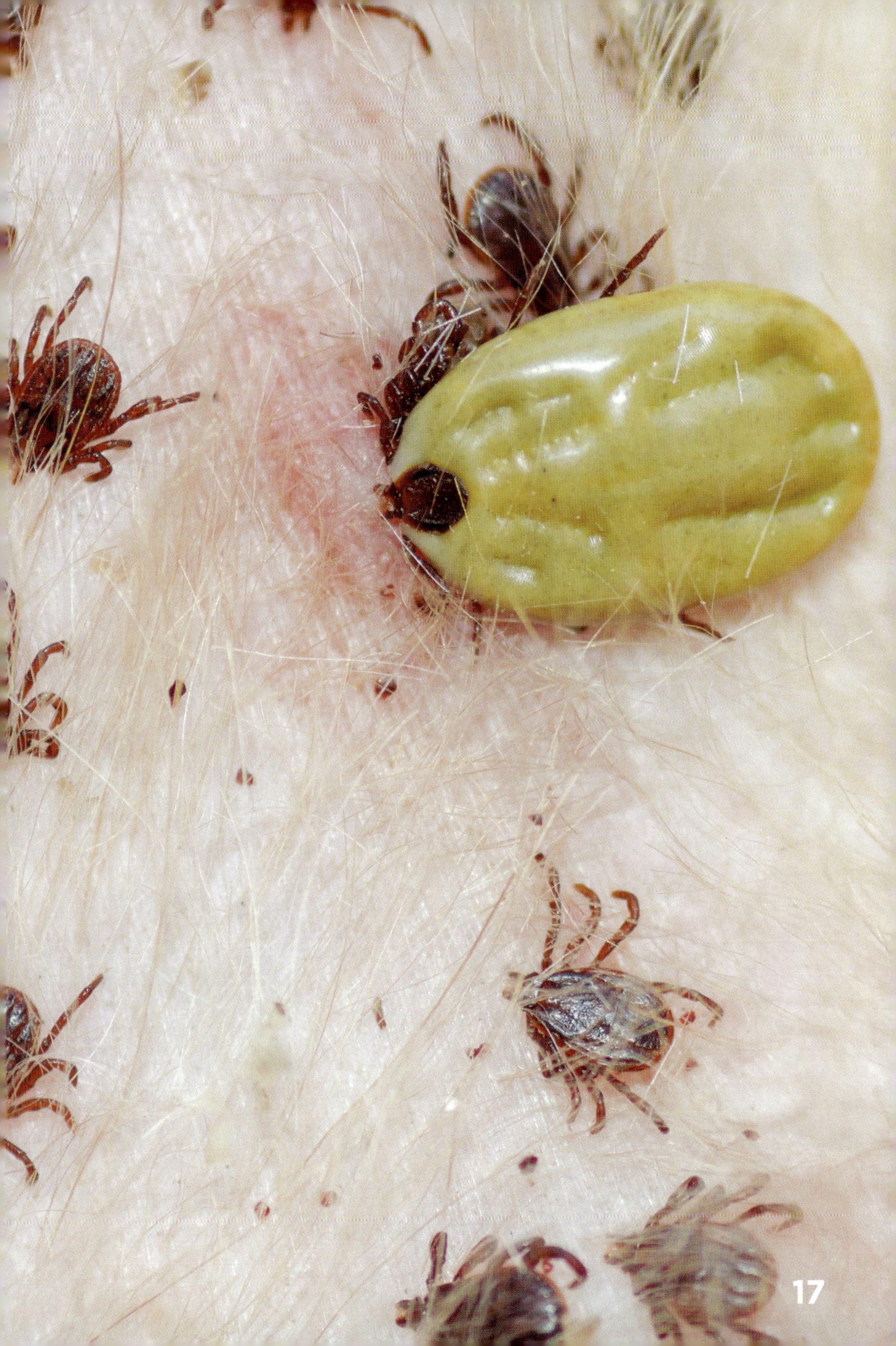

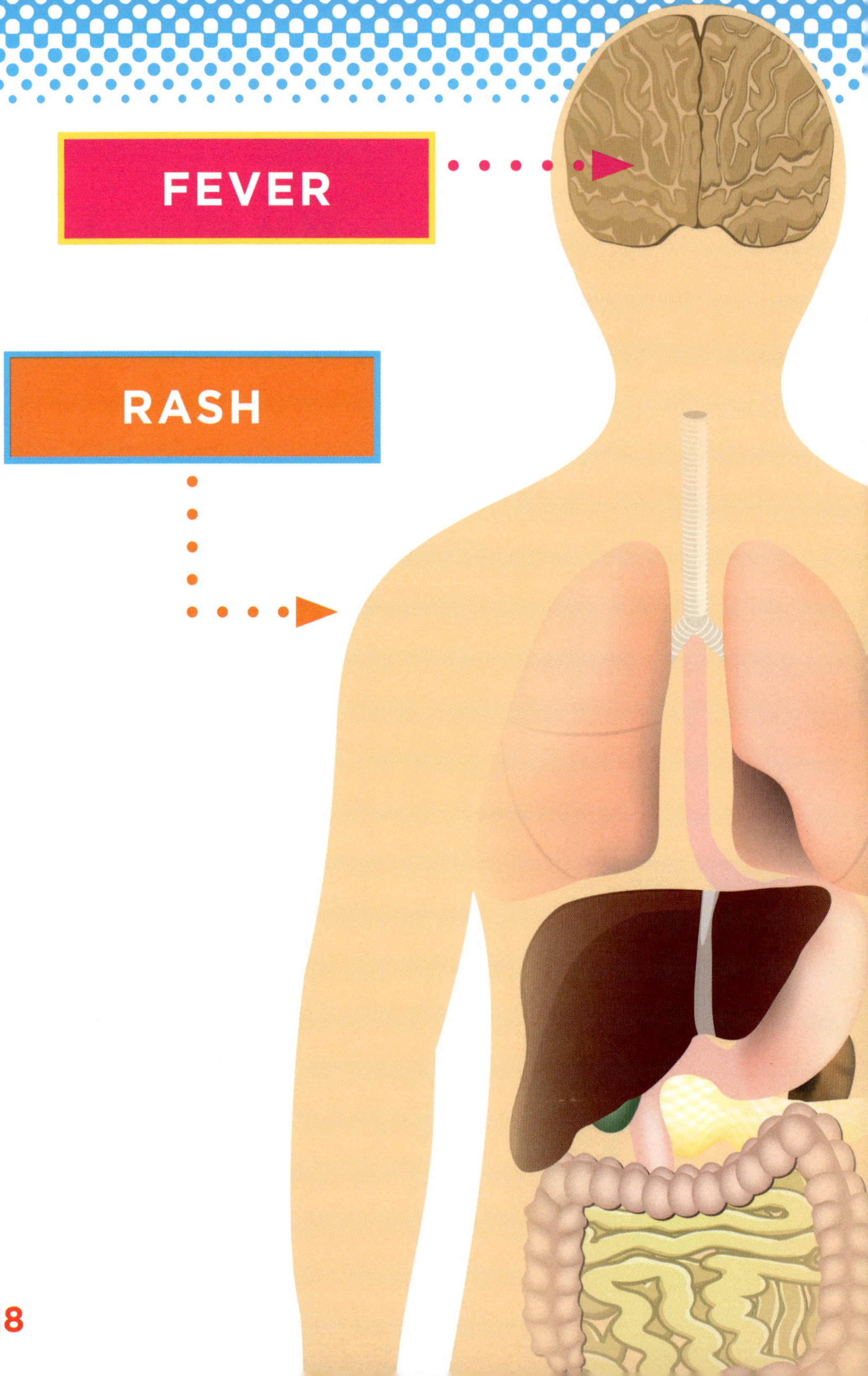
FEVER
RASH

Symptoms

Ticks can spread more than 15 different diseases. People might not feel a tick bite. But days after the bite, they might feel sick. Without treatment, the diseases can be deadly.

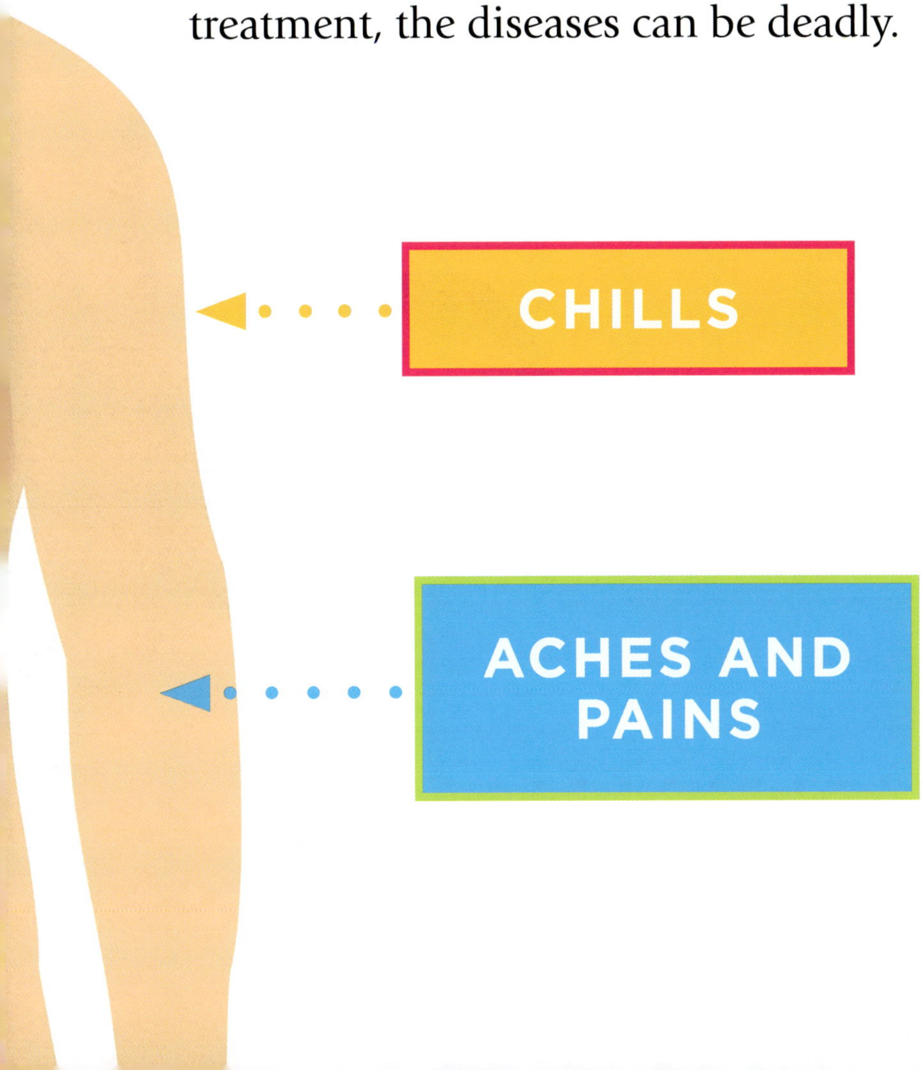

Lyme Disease

Lyme disease is one of the most common **tick-borne** illnesses in North America. It can spread to the heart and brain. Watch for a rash shaped like a bull's eye.

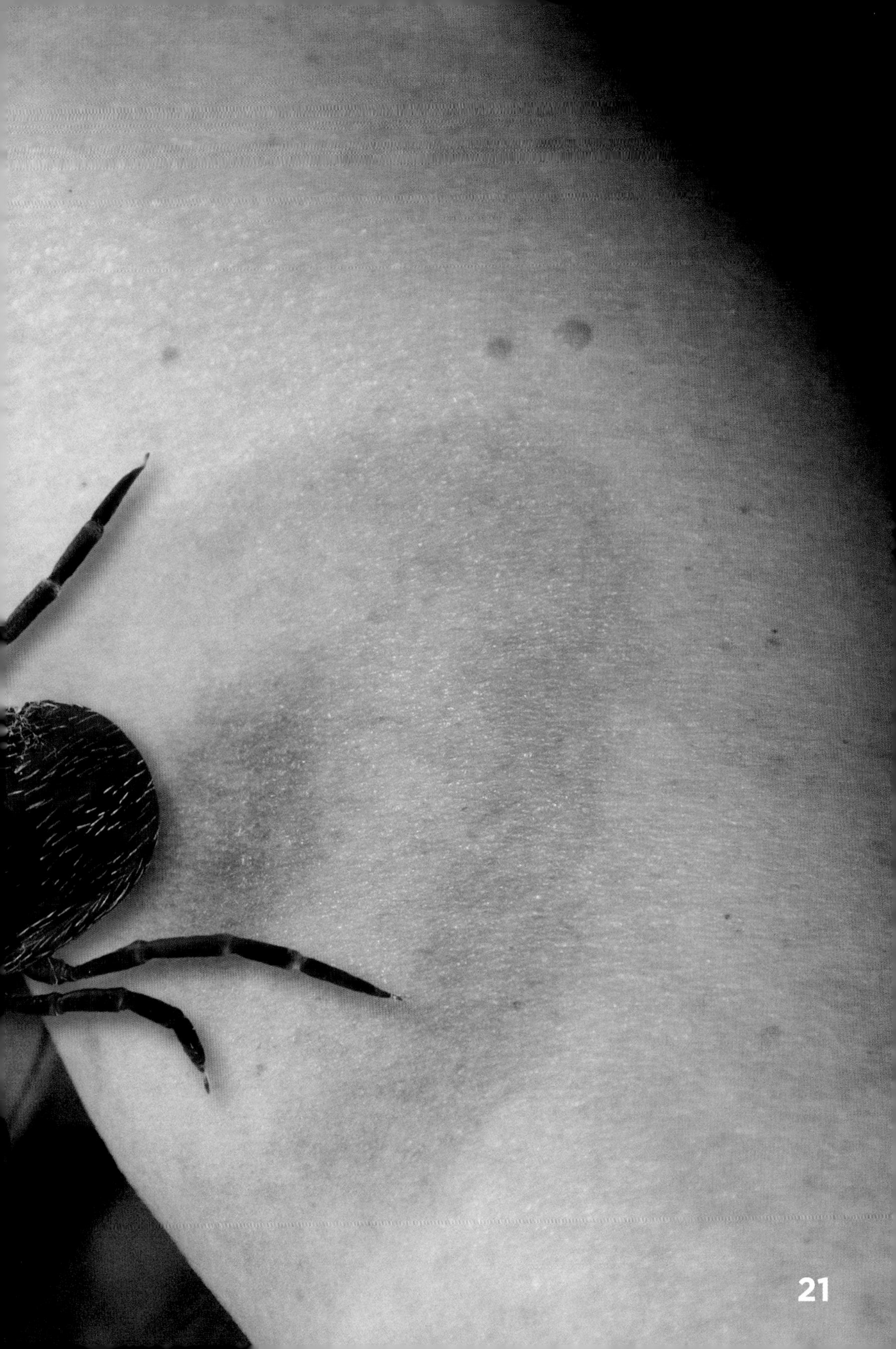

CHAPTER 4

Taking Control of Ticks

Ticks can be scary, but many are harmless. Only some ticks bite and give diseases to humans.

There are ways to prevent tick bites. When hiking and playing outside, avoid areas with tall grass. Afterward, carefully check for ticks hiding on the body.

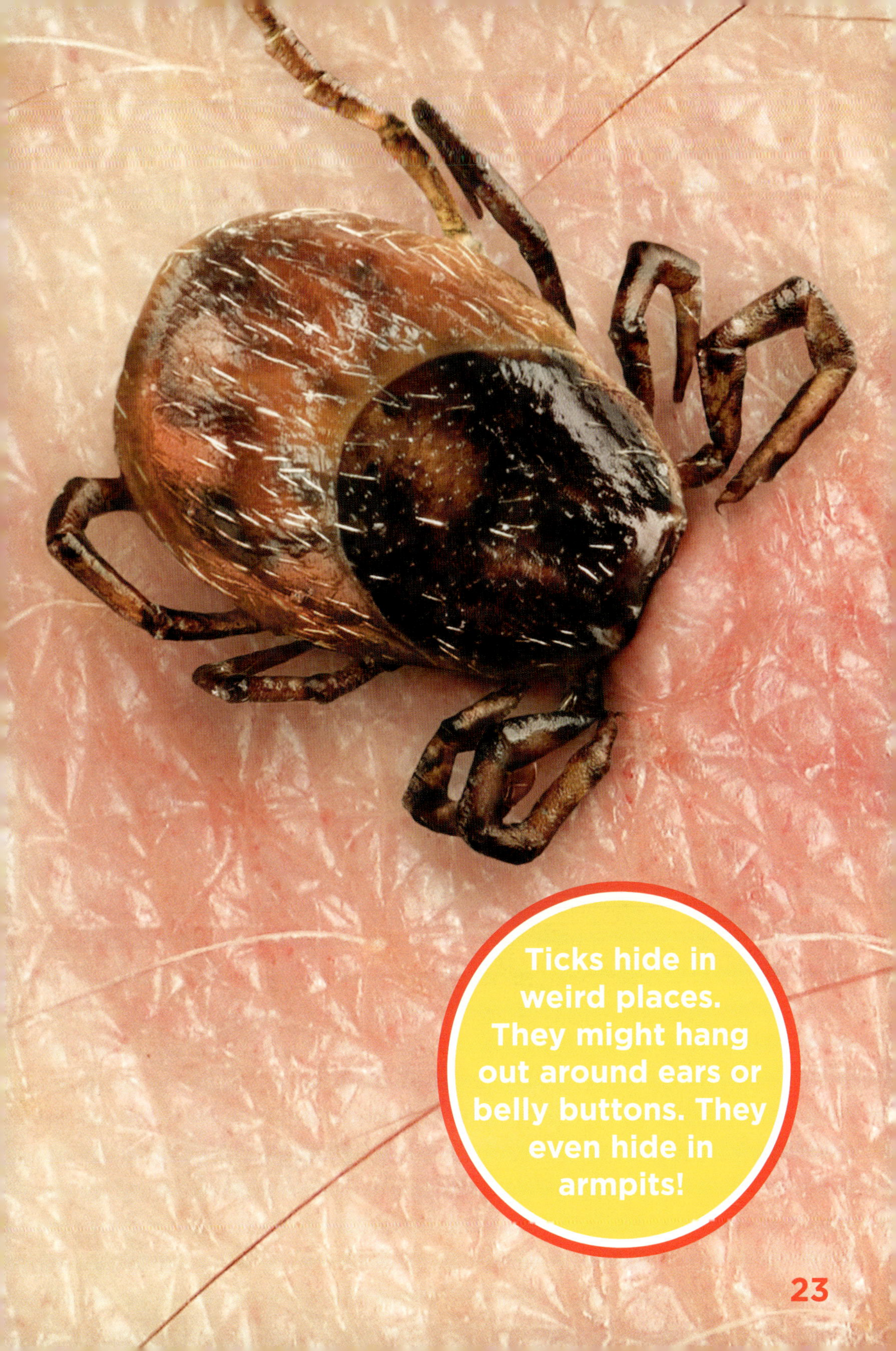

Ticks hide in weird places. They might hang out around ears or belly buttons. They even hide in armpits!

By the Numbers

200
number of days some ticks can go without eating

0.1 INCH (2.5 millimeters)

AVERAGE LENGTH OF AN UNFED ADULT FEMALE TICK

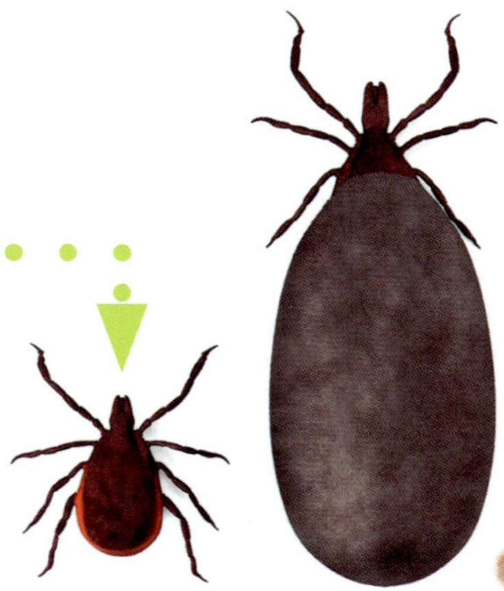

0.4 INCH (10 millimeters)

AVERAGE LENGTH OF AN ADULT FEMALE TICK AFTER A BLOOD MEAL

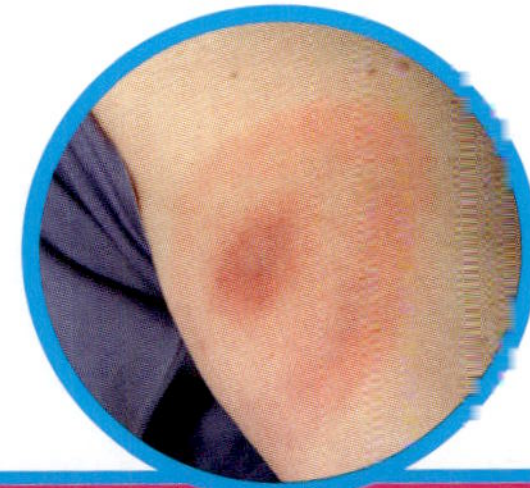

30,000

NUMBER OF CASES OF LYME DISEASE REPORTED EACH YEAR IN THE UNITED STATES

3,000 to 6,000

number of eggs an adult female tick lays

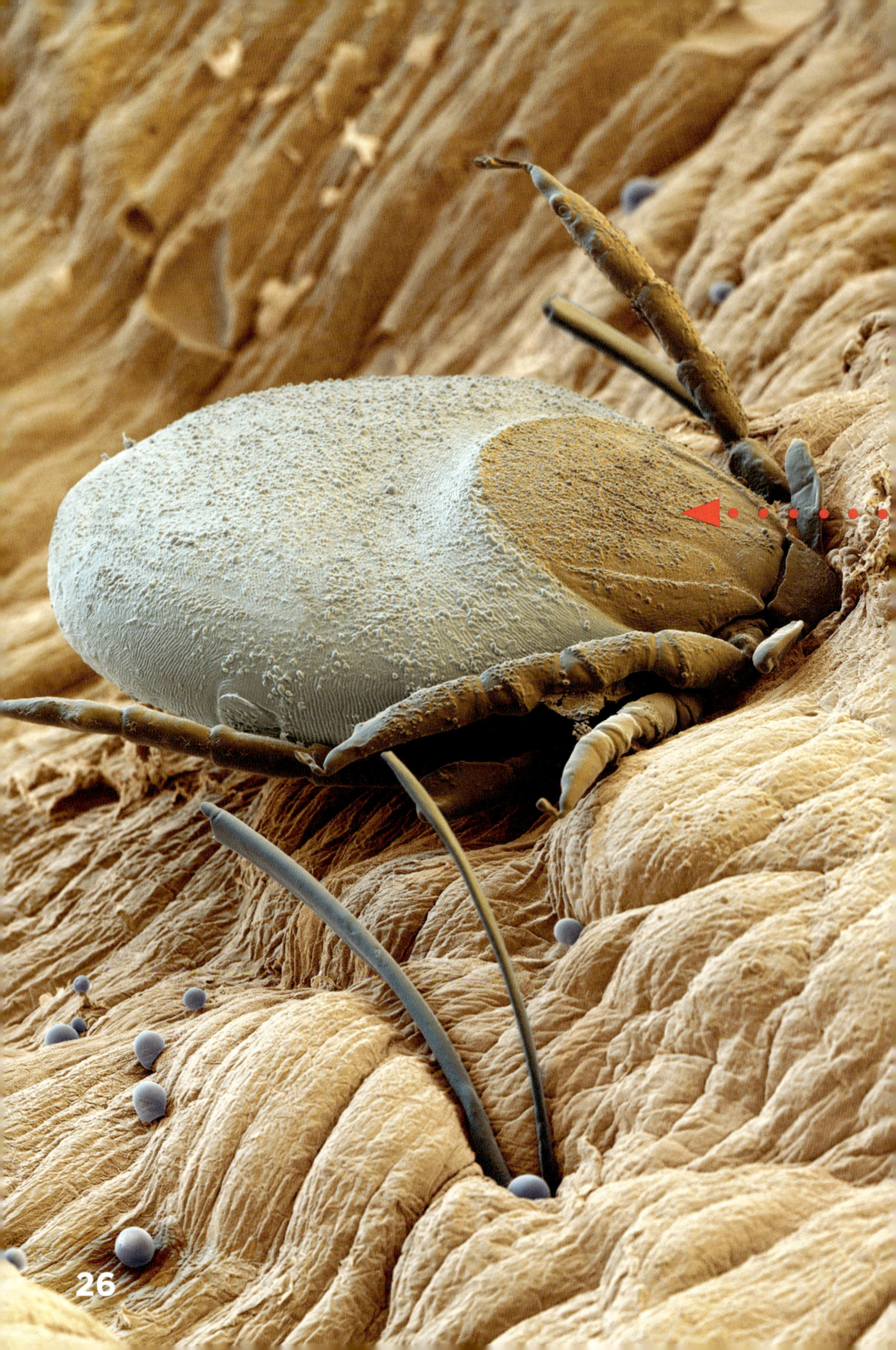

Tricky Ticks

Ticks are bloodthirsty parasites. They grab their victims and hold on tight. They live all over the world. They might even live in your backyard. Stay alert to defeat those tricky ticks!

Ticks can drink up to 600 times their body weight in blood.

Dino Snacks

Ticks have been around for millions of years. Scientists think ticks might have snacked on dinosaurs.

o Way!

arachnid (uh-RAK-nid)—a class of animals including spiders, scorpions, mites, and ticks

exoskeleton (ek-so-SKE-le-ten)—the hard, protective cover on the outside of an insect's or arachnid's body

larva (LAR-vuh)—the wormlike form of an animal after hatching from an egg

parasite (PAR-uh-syt)—a plant or animal that lives in or on another plant or animal and gets its food or protection from it

spine (SPYN)—a sharp, pointed part on an animal or plant

tick-borne (TIK-born)—describes something carried by a tick, such as a disease

LEARN MORE

BOOKS

Bodden, Valerie. *Ticks.* Creepy Creatures. Mankato, MN: Creative Education, 2013.

Faulk, Michelle. *The Case of the Infected Tick.* Body System Disease Investigations. New York: Enslow Publishers, 2013.

Fox, Nancy. *Hide-and-Seek: No Ticks, Please.* New York: Morgan James Pub., 2014.

WEBSITES

Deer Ticks
animals.nationalgeographic.com/animals/bugs/deer-tick/

Hey! A Tick Bit Me!
www.kidshealth.org/kid/watch/out/tick.html

Ticks
www.pestworldforkids.org/pest-guide/ticks/

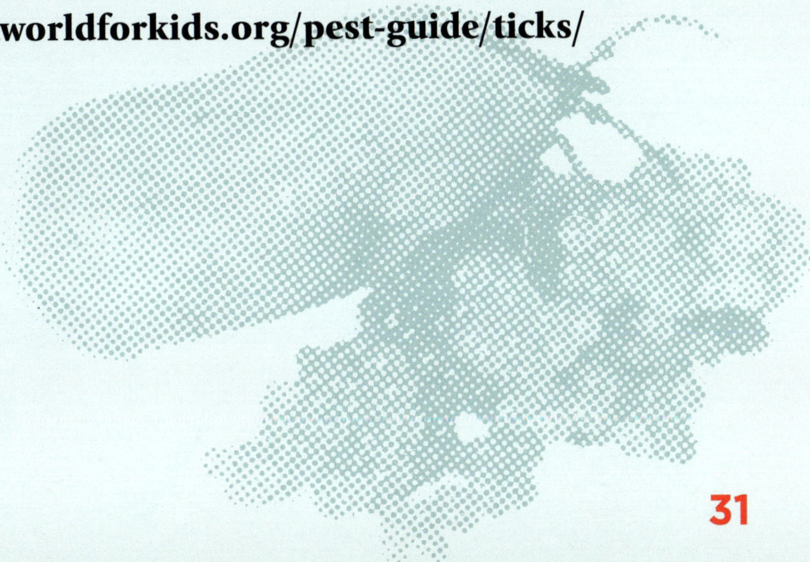

INDEX